Three Dimensional Patchwork™ *Sampler*

Jackie Robinson

Animas Quilts

Three Dimensional Patchwork™

Copyright © 1998
Jackie Robinson
Animas Quilts
600 Main Ave.
Durango, CO 81301
(970) 247-2582
http://www.animas.com
AnimasQuilts@Animas.com

Printed on Recycled Paper

ISBN: 1-885156-29-4

Three Dimensional Patchwork™ Sampler

Jackie Robinson

The author of ten books about patchwork, Jackie lives near Durango, in the southwest corner of Colorado. She and husband Jery Wyatt own Animas Quilts, a well known quilt shop which has been featured as one of America's top quilt shops in the American Patchwork & Quilting's Sampler and as one of the shops in That Patchwork Place's Top Shop series of books.

The mother of two grown children, Jackie teaches quilt making internationally, and attributes her ability to travel so much to the terrific staff that maintains daily life at Animas Quilts. She is known for her clear, easy to follow instructions, as well as for the warm humor she brings into the classroom.

About Three Dimensional Patchwork™

Three Dimensional Patchwork™ is a fun new way to fold and piece fabric, catching only the edges in the seams, leaving raised parts and creating 3-D Patchwork™. It's like popcorn - you just won't want to stop!

This text begins with a glossary of Three Dimensional Patchwork™ folds. The instructions are generic, with proportions defined, but without specific cut sizes, as those will change from unit to unit. Following the fold glossary, there is a section of patchwork blocks using Three Dimensional Patchwork™ folds. Each is presented as a 12" (finished) block, and includes specific cutting sizes for every part, as well as the folds used, and the sequence for construction.

Select the blocks for your Three Dimensional Patchwork™ Sampler and enjoy the process of discovering how much fun these techniques are. Once you've built the blocks, you'll find construction information at the end of the book for setting them in either a Straight or an On-Point set.

Yardage for these quilts:

This quilt being a Sampler, the yardage depends on the assortment of blocks and colors you choose. A general, and safe, rule of thumb is to purchase 1/3 yard of Background for every two blocks. This is generous, but 1/4 yard is not quite enough. And I've not yet met a quilter who's upset with having too much fabric!

The Colors used are bits of this and that. The amounts are very similar to the Background - each 1/3 yard of fabric (combined total) will make approximately two blocks. Use a large variety of fabrics for a more lively effect. When in doubt, add more! (Note: save some matching fabric for the setting stars, the amounts for which are shown with the "setting" information.)

The final section of this book is the "setting" information (see page 27). Select the set you desire and you'll find yardage requirements for putting your blocks together into a terrific Three Dimensional Patchwork™ Sampler quilt.

Basic construction info:

The blocks are constructed with 2 types of seams: *Security seams* and *Construction seams*. *Security seams* are narrow, about 1/8". Their purpose is to hold the assorted layers of fabric together so they are easy to handle during construction. When sewing a *Security seam*, you'll ALWAYS be looking at only the right sides of the fabrics. *Construction seams* are the typical scant 1/4" seams which are used to join the pieces of the block. When sewing a *Construction seam*, you'll ALWAYS be looking at the wrong sides of the fabric.

Take time to accurately check your *Construction seam*. I've found that a *scant 1/4" seam* (2 threads of fabric less than a full 1/4") works best. When you consider that the thread of the seam takes a little space, and the "fold over" of the fabric at that seam also takes some space, it's easy to understand that by sewing a full 1/4" seam, you'll end up using somewhat more than that, which then makes the finished size of your blocks smaller.

Pressing with an iron is not advised; it will smash the 3-D effect. Simply finger press and steam. I tend to add steam on the underside of the blocks at the seams, then with my fingers work it in so the seams are directed as desired. This way the 3-D Patchwork™ parts of the blocks aren't smashed.

Note: The quilt on the Front Cover uses lamé. For ease in handling, bond tissue (not tricot!) lamé with woven fusible interfacing before cutting.

Let the folds begin!

Half Square Triangle. Fold a square of Color in half, diagonally, right side out. Place it on top of the right side of an equal size Background square, raw edges even and the fold across the center of the Background. Stitch a 1/8" security seam around the raw edges.

Double Half Square Triangles. Fold a square of Color A in half diagonally, right side out. Place it on top of the right side of an equal size Background square, raw edges even and the fold across the center of the Background. Fold a smaller square of Color B in half diagonally, right side out. Position it exactly on top of the Color A triangle. Stitch a 1/8" security seam around the raw edges.

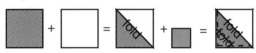

Overlapping Half Square Triangles. Fold a square of Color A in half diagonally, right side out. Place it on top of the right side of an equal size Background square, raw edges even and the fold across the center of the Background. Fold a equal size square of Color B in half diagonally, right side out. Position it to overlap half of the Color A triangle. Stitch a 1/8" security seam around the raw edges.

Pieced Half Square Triangle. Create a "traditional" half-square triangle unit by sewing two right triangles together along their long edges.

Fold this pieced unit in half diagonally, right side out. Place it on top of the right side of an equal size Background square, raw edges even and the fold across the center of the Background. Stitch a 1/8" security seam around the raw edges.

Snowball Corner. A snowball corner is a half-square triangle variation where the foundation Background piece is larger than the folded piece. Fold a square of Color in half diagonally, right side out. Place it on top of the right side of a larger sized Background square or rectangle, raw edges even and the fold toward the center of the Background. Stitch a 1/8" security seam around the raw edges.

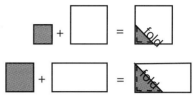

Double Snowball Corners. Fold a square of Color in half diagonally, right side out. Place it on top of the right side of a larger sized Background square or rectangle, raw edges even and the fold toward the center of the Background. Fold a second square of Color in half diagonally, right side out. Place it adjacent to or opposite the previous square, depending on the desired positioning. Stitch a 1/8" security seam around the raw edges.

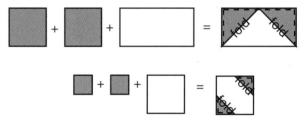

Flying Geese. A goose is made from a rectangle that is twice as long as it is wide, plus 1/2" for seam allowances (i.e. 2-1/2" x 4-1/2" OR 3-1/2" x 6-1/2") and two squares of Background equal to the smaller measurement.

Fold the rectangle of Color in half, right side out, making it almost square. Place it on the right side of a square that equals the rectangle's smaller measurement. All the raw edges must be together across the top, and the fold of the goose will be 1/4" above the lower raw edge of the Background square.

Place a second Background square on top of the goose rectangle, right side down. Again, all raw edges are equal across the top edge, and the goose piece is sandwiched between the Background squares. Stitch along the right side with a scant 1/4" seam.

Open out the Background squares and spread open the goose rectangle to form a 3-D Flying Goose. Run a 1/8" Security seam across the wingspread.

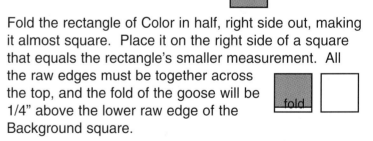

3

Nose to Nose Geese. This pair of geese is made from four equal rectangles (two of Color and two of Background) which are twice as long as they are wide, plus 1/2" for seam allowances. (i.e. 2-1/2" x 4-1/2" OR 3-1/2" x 6-1/2")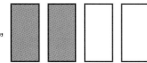

Fold a rectangle of Color in half, right side out, making it almost square. Place it on the right side of a Background rectangle, lining it up so the raw edges are even at the top and the fold of the Color rectangle is in the middle of the Background rectangle. Fold a second rectangle of Color in half, right side out, making it almost square. Place it directly below the first rectangle of Color, with the folded edges just meeting, but not overlapping. This will put the raw edges of the second Color rectangle even with the Background along the bottom. Place a second Background rectangle on top of the folded geese rectangles, right side down. Again, all raw edges are equal, and the geese pieces are sandwiched between the Background rectangles. Stitch along the right side with a scant 1/4" seam.

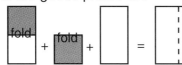

Open out the Background rectangles and spread open the folded geese rectangles to form a pair of nose to nose 3-D geese. Run a 1/8" Security seam across both wing spreads.

Two Geese in a Row. This pair of geese is made from three equal rectangles (two of Color and one of Background) which are twice as long as they are wide, plus 1/2" for seam allowances (i.e. 2-1/2" x 4-1/2" OR 3-1/2" x 6-1/2") and two squares of Background the measurement of the rectangle's short side.

Fold a rectangle of Color in half, right side out, making it almost square. Place it on the right side of a Background square, lining it up so the raw edges are even and the fold of the Color rectangle is 1/4" above the lower edge of the Background square.

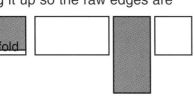

Place the Background rectangle horizontally on top of the folded goose rectangle, right side down. Top and right raw edges are

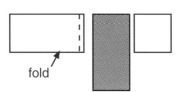

equal, and the goose pieces are sandwiched between the Background rectangle and square. Stitch along the right side with a scant 1/4" seam.

Open out the Backgrounds and place a second folded goose rectangle on the remaining corner. Position a Background square right side down on top, forming a sandwich. Stitch along the right edge with a scant 1/4" seam.

Spread open the goose rectangles to form a pair of side by side 3-D geese. Run a 1/8" Security seam across both wing spreads.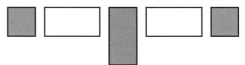

Goose with Snowballs. This goose is made from three equal rectangles (one of Color A and two of Background) which are twice as long as they are wide, plus 1/2" for seam allowance (i.e. 2-1/2" x 4-1/2" OR 3-1/2" x 6-1/2") and two squares of Color B equal in size to the short side of the rectangles.

Fold a rectangle of Color A in half, right side out, making it almost square. Place it on the right side of a Background rectangle, lining it up so the raw edges are even and the fold of the Color A rectangle is 1/4" above the lower edge of the Background rectangle.

Place the second Background rectangle on top of the folded geese rectangles, right side down. Again, top and right raw edges are equal, and the goose piece is sandwiched between the Background rectangles. Stitch along the right side with a scant 1/4" seam.

Open out the Background rectangles and spread open the goose rectangle to form a 3-D goose.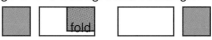

Fold a square of Color B in half diagonally, right side out. Place it on a bare corner of the Background rectangle. Likewise, place another folded square of Color B on the remaining corner of Background. Run a 1/8" Security seam around both corners and across the wing spread.

Flying Goose with a Star Point. This goose made from three equal rectangles (Color A, Color B, and Background) which are twice as long as they are wide, plus 1/2" for seam allowances (i.e. 2-1/2" x 4-1/2" OR 3-1/2" x 6-1/2") and a square of Background equal to the short side of the rectangles.

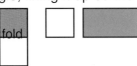

Fold a rectangle of Color A in half, right side out, like a flying goose, making it almost square. Place it on the right side of a Background rectangle, lining it up so the raw edges are even and the fold of the Color A rectangle is in the middle of the Background rectangle.

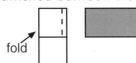

Place a Background square on top of the folded goose rectangle, right side down. Again, all raw edges are equal, and the goose piece is sandwiched between the Background rectangle and square. Stitch along the right side with a scant 1/4" seam.

Open out the Background and spread open the goose rectangle to form a 3-D goose. Run a 1/8" Security seam across the wing spread.

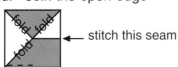

Place a same size rectangle of Color B (for star point) right side down, perpendicular, on top of the rectangular piece of Background extending beyond the goose. Before stitching, fold back the Color B piece 45° at the corner. Stitch with a 1/8" Security seam along the short edge of the Background. Join the open edge where Color B meets the Background square under the goose.

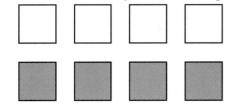

— stitch this seam

Prairie Point Pinwheel. Each Pinwheel requires four squares of Color and four squares of Background.

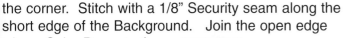

Fold a square of Color in half, diagonally, right side out. Fold it a second time, diagonally. Place the folded Color piece along a right side up edge of a same size Background square, positioning it so the open fold of the Color is toward the lower edge of the Background. Attach with a narrow 1/8" Security seam.

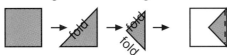

Make four of each color and join with scant 1/4" seams in a 4-patch to create a pinwheel. When stitching the final cross seam of the 4-patch, be mindful of the direction the Prairie Point needs to be facing, and direct the seams so they not only face opposite directions, but also keep the Prairie Point Pinwheel lying properly. If you've laid your pinwheel out exactly like ours, the seam allowance closest to you will slide away from the needle, while the under seam allowance will be aimed toward the back of your machine. On the underside, clip on the seam allowance AT the seam allowance in the center and 'spin' the seams.

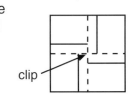

clip

Note: If the extra layers have a tendency to shift with the pressure of the presser foot, begin stitching about 3/8" down from the top and they won't shift.

Bow Tie Knot. This fold requires five equal squares of fabric - three of the tie Color and two of Background.

Fold a square of Color in half, horizontally, right side out. Place it on top of the right side of another square of the same Color, matching raw edges. The fold will be lying across the middle of the under square.

Place a square of background on top of the two Color pieces, right side down, lining up raw edges. Stitch with a scant 1/4" seam along the right edge, catching all four layers at the beginning of that seam, and ending with only the two layers.

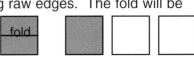

fold

Open out this piece and hold it by the folded piece with the two attached squares "dangling" off the the left. Place this folded piece on top of a square of Color, right side up, keeping all the raw edges even across the top and in the upper right corner. Place a square of Background on top of this grouping, right side toward the folded piece. Sew a scant 1/4" seam along the right edge.

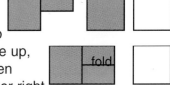

Spread the folded Color section and in the process, bring the two seams together at the top, sandwiching the folded center Color piece between. Stitch across the top with a scant 1/4" seam. Open the block to find the Bow Tie with a 3-D knot.

On Point Center Square. Like the Bow Tie, this block requires five squares of fabric. However, the proportions are different. The four Background squares are all the same size. The Center Color square is twice the width and length of the Background squares, adjusted with seam allowances. (i.e. 3-1/2" Background squares and a 6-1/2" Center square OR 2-1/2" Background squares and 4-1/2" Center square)

Fold the large square of Color in half horizontally, right side out. Sandwich it between two squares of Background, their right side facing the Color. Line up the raw edges. The fold of the Color will be 1/4" short of the lower edge of the Background squares. Stitch with a scant 1/4" seam along the side edge, catching the raw edges and the fold.

Likewise, sandwich the opposite edge of the folded Center Color between two more squares of Background. Stitch along the side with a scant 1/4" seam.

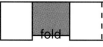

Open the 'pocket' formed in the Center Color fabric. Spread it so the two seams just stitched come together. Stitch across this edge, catching the sandwiched Center Color piece in the seam. Open, and there's an On Point Center Square.

Center Square with Geese. This unit is made from two rectangles of Color B for the geese, four rectangles of the same size of Background and a square equal to the long side of the goose of Color A.

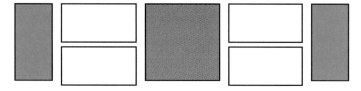

Fold the large square of Color A in half, horizontally, right side out. Sandwich each end between the right sides of two Background rectangles, along their short sides. Stitch each side with a scant 1/4" seam.

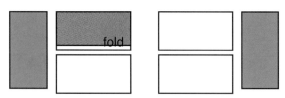

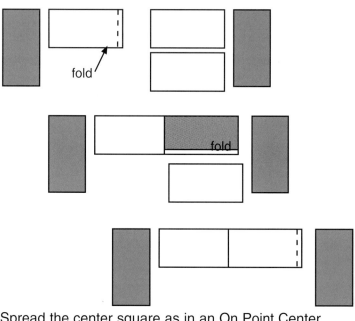

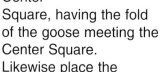

Spread the center square as in an On Point Center Square. Before stitching, fold a rectangle of Color B (goose) in half, vertically, right side out. Place it between the "empty" ends beyond the Center Square, having the fold of the goose meeting the Center Square. Likewise place the remaining Color B goose rectangle at the other end. Stitch across all with a scant 1/4" seam. The Center Square will be in place. Add 1/8" Security seams to hold the geese wing spreads in place.

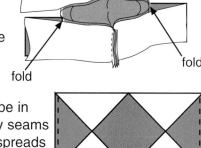

Star Points. These are generally a mirror image pair made with two rectangles of Color and two same sized rectangles of Background. The rectangles are twice as long as they are wide, plus seam allowance.

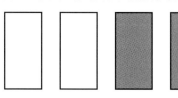

Fold under one corner of a Color rectangle 45° and place the Color exactly on top of the right side of the same size Background rectangle. Stitch a 1/8" Security seam around all three sides to hold it in place. Likewise, make a mirror-image star point. Finally, stitch the pair together with a scant 1/4" seam.

Star Points with Snowball Corners. These units are exactly like Star Points EXCEPT a square of selected fabric is folded in half diagonally, right side out, and placed on top of the Color. Security stitch to hold in place, and join the two parts with a scant 1/4" seam.

Crocus with Snowballs. The pieces needed are a Background rectangle which is twice as long as wide, a square of Color A equal to the longest measurement of the rectangle, and two squares of Color B equal in size to the smallest side of the rectangle.

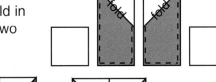

Fold the large square of Color A in half diagonally, right side out. Fold it in half again. Place the long edge even with the long edge of the Background rectangle. Secure in place with a single pin.

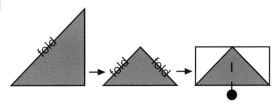

Fold a smaller square of Color B in half, diagonally, right side out. Place on top of the corner of the large Point and Background. Likewise, fold a second square of Color B and place it on the opposite corner. Security stitch a 1/8" seam allowance around the three sides.

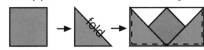

Tulip Tip. This fold requires three small squares of Color A, two small squares of Background, one small square of Color B, and a larger square of Color A which is twice the width and length of the smaller ones.

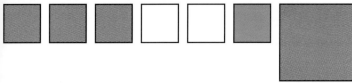

Fold a small square of Color A in half, diagonally, right side out, and place it on top of a Background square. Secure stitch a 1/8" seam. Make two.

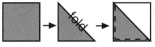

Assemble a 4-patch using these two units plus another square of Color A and a square of Color B, sewing with scant 1/4" seams.

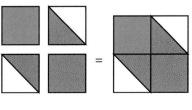

Fold the larger square of Color A in half, diagonally, right side out, and place it on top of the 4-patch unit just made, positioning so the larger triangle is over the corner of the same color. Stitch a 1/8" Security seam around the edges.

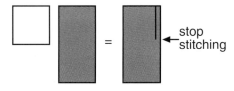

Short Sheet Fold. Vertically place a rectangle which is twice as long as it is wide (plus seam allowance) of Color on top of a square of Background (equal to the short measurement of the rectangle), right sides together, with the two fabrics lined up at the top. Stitch down the side with a scant 1/4" seam, stopping the stitching 1/4" from the edge of the Background square at the center.

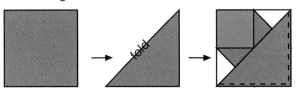

Pick up the lower edge of the Color piece just sewn and open it toward the right, diagonally. This creates a diagonal fold on top of the Background. Stitch a narrow 1/8" Security stitch along the top edge.

SPECIAL THANKS TO:

Debbie Austin, Theodore, Queensland, Australia for simplifying Nose to Nose Geese

Suzan Drury, Sedona, AZ for Pieced Half Square Triangles

Mary Ellen Hopkins, Santa Monica, CA and Jan Krueger, Hales Corners, WI for showing me 3-D Flying Geese

And now - the blocks:

Each block is presented as a 12" finished block. Take care with seam allowances and accurate cutting. Each should measure 12-1/2" in its raw form. Remember to steam, more than press, if you do not want to smash the 3-D effect.

Arrowpoint

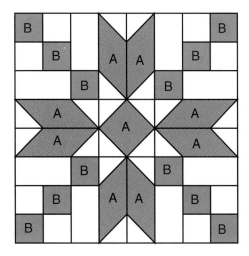

Color A
(1) 3-1/2" sq.
(8) 2" x 5"

Color B
(12) 2" sq.

Background
(8) 2" x 5"
(20) 2" sq.
(8) 2" x 3-1/2"

Folds Used:
Star Points with Snowball Corners
On Point Center Square

Sequence:
1. Build (4) 9-patch corners with Color B squares and 2" squares of Background plus 2" x 3-1/2" Backgrounds.

2. Make (4) Star Point with Snowball Corners in mirror image using 2" x 5" Color A on top of 2" x 5" Backgrounds. Place Half-square folds of 2" square Backgrounds on top for Snowball Corners.

3. Make an On Point Center Square of the 3-1/2" square Color A between 2" squares of Background.

4. Assemble the block.

Aunt Sukey's Choice

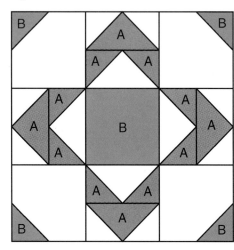

Color A
(4) 2-1/2" x 4-1/2"
(8) 2-1/2" sq.

Color B
(1) 4-1/2" sq.
(4) 2-1/2" sq.

Background
(4) 4-1/2" sq.
(4) 2-1/2" x 4-1/2"
(8) 2-1/2" sq.

Folds used:
Snowball Corners
Double Snowball Corners
Flying Goose

Sequence:
1. Make (4) Snowball Corners using 2-1/2" squares of Color B on top of 4-1/2" squares of Background.

2. Make (4) Double Snowball Corners with 2-1/2" squares of Color A on top of 2-1/2" x 4-1/2" Backgrounds.

3. Make (4) Flying Goose units using 2-1/2" x 4-1/2" Color A between 2-1/2" squares Background.

4. Assemble the block.

Bird's Nest

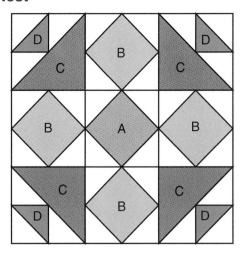

Color A
(1) 4-1/2" sq.

Color B
(4) 4-1/2" sq.

Color C
(4) 4-1/2" sq.

Color D
(4) 2-1/2" sq.

Background
(4) 2-1/2" x 4-1/2"
(28) 2-1/2" sq.

Folds Used:
Half Square Triangles
On Point Center Squares

Sequence:
1. Make (5) On Point Center Squares using one 4-1/2" square of Color A and four 4-1/2" squares of Color B between 2-1/2" squares Background.

2. Make (4) Half Square Triangles using 2-1/2" squares of Color D on top of 2-1/2" squares Background.

3. Join each of the Color D Half-Square Triangles to a 2-1/2" square of Background, then to a 2-1/2" x 4-1/2" Background.

4. Make (4) Half Square Triangles using 4-1/2" squares of Color C on top of the units made in Step 3.

5. Assemble the block.

Bow Tie

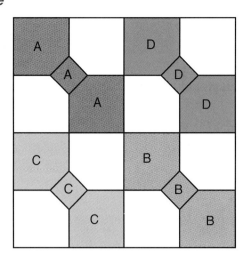

Color A
(3) 3-1/2" sq.

Color B
(3) 3-1/2" sq.

Color C
(3) 3-1/2" sq.

Color D
(3) 3-1/2" sq.

Background
(8) 3-1/2" sq.

Folds used:
Bow Tie

Sequence:
1. Make (4) Bow Tie Units, one of each color, with the Color square sandwiched between squares of Color and Background.

2. Assemble the block.

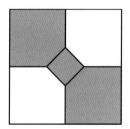

Broken Window

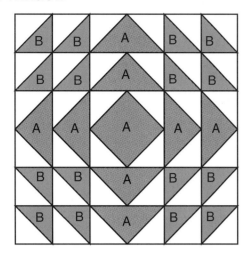

Color A
(1) 4-1/2" sq.
(8) 2-1/2" x 4-1/2"

Color B
(16) 2-1/2" sq.

Background
(36) 2-1/2" sq.

Folds used:
Half Square Triangle
Flying Goose
On Point Center Square

Sequence:
1. Make (8) Flying Geese using 2-1/2" x 4-1/2" Color A between 2-1/2" squares of Background.

2. Join the Geese in pairs, heading the same direction, with scant 1/4" seams.

3. Make (16) Half Square Triangles with 2-1/2" squares of Color B on top of 2-1/2" squares of Background.

4. Join (4) Half Square Triangles, facing the same direction, into (4) 4-patch units.

5. Make an On Point Center Square with a 4-1/2" square of Color A between 2-1/2" squares of Background.

6. Assemble the block.

Christmas Star

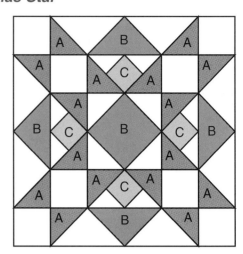

Color A
(16) 2-1/2" sq.

Color B
(1) 4-1/2" sq.
(4) 2-1/2" x 4-1/2"

Color C
(4) 4-1/2" sq.

Background
(12) 2-1/2" x 4-1/2"
(12) 2-1/2" sq.

Folds used:
On Point Center Square
Crocus with Snowballs
Goose with Snowballs

Sequence:
1. Make an On Point Center Square with a 4-1/2" square Color B between 2-1/2" squares of Background.

2. Make (4) Crocus with Snowballs of 4-1/2" squares Color C and then 2-1/2" squares of Color A on top of 2-1/2" x 4-1/2" Backgrounds.

3. Make (4) Goose with Snowballs using 2-1/2" x 4-1/2" Color B between 2-1/2" x 4-1/2" Backgrounds, and with 2-1/2" squares of Color A on top.

4. Assemble the block.

Cross and Crown

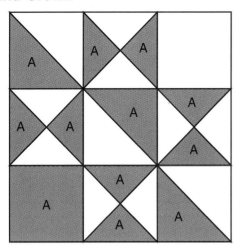

Color A
(4) 4-1/2" sq.
(8) 2-1/2" x 4-1/2"

Background
(4) 4-1/2" sq.
(8) 2-1/2" x 4-1/2"

Folds used:
Half Square Triangle
Nose to Nose Geese

Sequence:
1. Make (2) Nose to Nose Geese with 2-1/2" x 4-1/2" Color A sandwiched between 2-1/2" x 4-1/2" Backgrounds.

2. Make (2) Nose to Nose Geese with 2-1/2" x 4-1/2" Backgrounds sandwiched between 2-1/2" x 4-1/2" Color A.

3. Make (3) Half Square Triangles with a 4-1/2" square Color A on top of a 4-1/2" square of Background.

4. Assemble the block with the raised parts of the Nose to Nose Geese forming the star points.

Devil's Claws

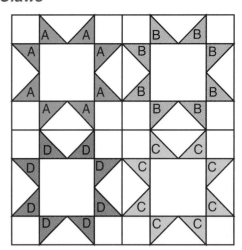

Color A
(8) 2" sq.

Color B
(8) 2" sq.

Color C
(8) 2" sq.

Color D
(8) 2" sq.

Background
(4) 3-1/2" sq.
(16) 2" x 3-1/2"
(16) 2" sq.

Folds Used:
Double Snowball Corners

Sequence:
1. Make (4) Double Snowball Corners of 2-1/2" squares of each Color on top of 2" x 3-1/2" Backgrounds.

2. Assemble each star, placing a 3-1/2" square of Background in each center.

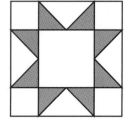

3. Assemble the block.

Dutchman's Puzzle

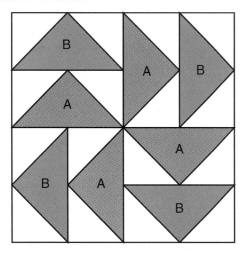

Color A
(4) 3-1/2" x 6-1/2"

Color B
(4) 3-1/2" x 6-1/2"

Background
(16) 3-1/2" sq.

Folds used:
Flying Goose

Sequence:
1. Make (4) Flying Geese of
3-1/2" x 6-1/2" Color A between
3-1/2" squares of Background.

2. Make (4) Flying Geese of
3-1/2" x 6-1/2" Color B between
3-1/2" squares of Background.

3. Join a Color A Goose and a
Color B Goose facing the same
direction, Color B pointing outward,
with a scant 1/4" seam.

4. Assemble the block.

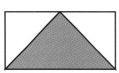

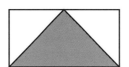

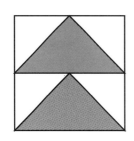

Eight-Pointed Star

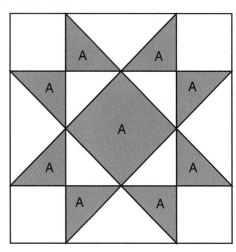

Color A
(1) 6-1/2" sq.
(8) 3-1/2" sq.

Background
(4) 3-1/2" x 6-1/2"
(8) 3-1/2" sq.

Folds used:
Double Snowball Corners
On Point Center Square

Sequence:
1. Make (4) Double Snowball
Corners with 3-1/2" squares of
Color A on top of 3-1/2" x 6-1/2"
Backgrounds.

2. Make an On Point Center
Square with a 6-1/2" square of
Color A between 3-1/2" squares
of Background.

3. Assemble the block.

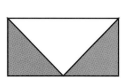

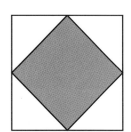

Fireworks Pinwheel

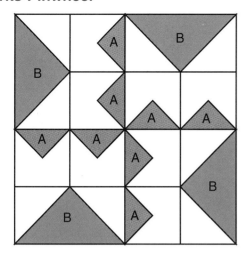

Color A
(8) 3-1/2" sq.

Color B
(4) 3-1/2" x 6-1/2"

Background
(16) 3-1/2" sq.

Folds used:
Flying Goose
Prairie Point Pinwheel

Sequence:
1. Make (4) Flying Geese with 3-1/2" x 6-1/2" Color B between 3-1/2" squares of Background.

2. Make (8) Pinwheel parts with 3-1/2" squares of Color A on top of 3-1/2" squares of Background.

3. Join the Pinwheel parts in side by side pairs.

4. Add a Goose to each pair of Pinwheel parts, point to point.

5. Assemble the block, being mindful of the direction of the Pinwheels.

6. Clip the center seam at the seam to 'spin' seam allowances.

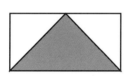

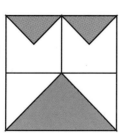

Flock of Geese

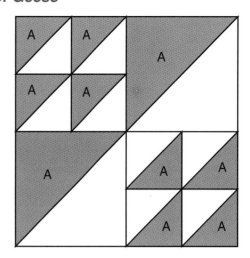

Color A
(2) 6-1/2" sq.
(8) 3-1/2" sq.

Background
(2) 6-1/2" sq.
(8) 3-1/2" sq.

Folds used:
Half Square Triangle

Sequence:
1. Make (4) Half Square Triangles with 3-1/2" squares of Color A on top of 3-1/2" squares of Background.

2. Sew these Step 1 Half Square Triangles together in a 4-patch.

3. Make (4) Half Square Triangles with 3-1/2" squares of Background on top of 3-1/2" squares of Color A.

4. Sew these Step 3 Half Square Triangles together in a 4-patch.

5. Make (2) Half Square Triangles with 6-1/2" squares of Background on top of 6-1/2" squares of Color A.

6. Assemble the block.

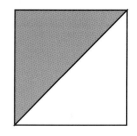

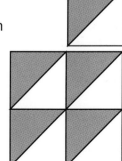

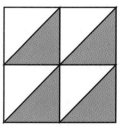

Flutter Wheel

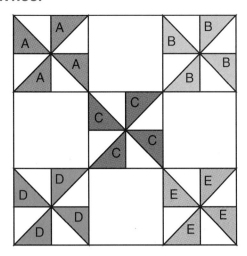

Fly Foot

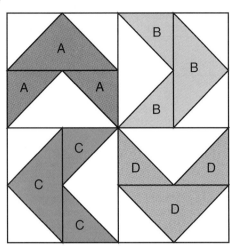

Color A
(4) 2-1/2" sq.

Color B
(4) 2-1/2" sq.

Color C
(4) 2-1/2" sq.

Color D
(4) 2-1/2" sq.

Color E
(4) 2-1/2" sq.

Background
(4) 4-1/2" sq.
(20) 2-1/2" sq.

Color A
(1) 3-1/2" x 6-1/2"
(2) 3-1/2" sq.

Color B
(1) 3-1/2" x 6-1/2"
(2) 3-1/2" sq.

Color C
(1) 3-1/2" x 6-1/2"
(2) 3-1/2" sq.

Color D
(1) 3-1/2" x 6-1/2"
(2) 3-1/2" sq.

Background
(4) 3-1/2" x 6-1/2"
(8) 3-1/2" sq.

Folds used:
Half Square Triangle

Folds used:
Double Snowball Corners
Flying Goose

Sequence:
1. Make (4) Half Square Triangles with 2-1/2" squares of each Color on top of 2-1/2" squares of Background.

2. Assemble (5) Flutter sections of four Half Square Triangles.

3. Assemble the block.

Sequence:
1. Make a Flying Goose of each 3-1/2" x 6-1/2" Color between 3-1/2" squares of Background.

2. Make a Double Snowball Corner with (2) 3-1/2" squares of each Color on top of 3-1/2" x 6-1/2" Backgrounds.

3. Join each Flying Goose to a Double Snowball Corner unit, being mindful of the direction they point, with a scant 1/4" seam.

4. Assemble the block.

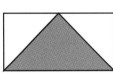

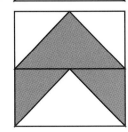

Four-Corner Puzzle

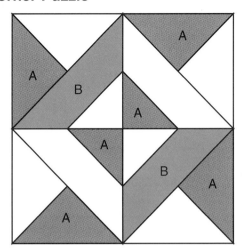

Color A
(4) 6-1/2" sq.
(2) 3-1/2" sq.

Color B
(2) 6-1/2" sq.

Background
(6) 6-1/2" sq.
(2) 3-1/2" sq.

Folds used:
Overlapping Half Square Triangles

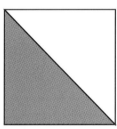

Sequence:
1. Make (4) Half Square Triangles with 6-1/2" squares of Color A on top of 6-1/2" squares of Background.

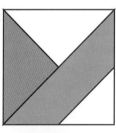

2. Make (2) Overlapping Half Square Triangles with 6-1/2" squares of Color B and then 3-1/2" squares of Background diagonally on top of the Step 1 unit.

3. Make (2) Overlapping Half Square Triangles with 6-1/2" squares of Background and then 3-1/2" squares of Color A diagonally on top of the Step 1 unit.

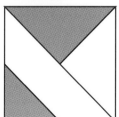

4. Assemble the block.

Gem

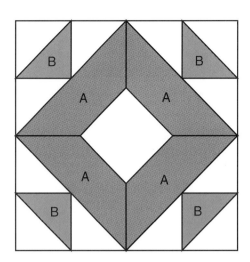

Color A
(4) 6-1/2" sq.

Color B
(4) 3-1/2" sq.

Background
(1) 6-1/2" sq.
(4) 3-1/2" x 6-1/2"
(8) 3-1/2" sq.

Folds used:
Half Square Triangle
On Point Center Square

Sequence:
1. Make (4) Half Square Triangles with 3-1/2" squares of Color B on top of 3-1/2" squares of Background.

2. Join each of these Half Square Triangles to a 3-1/2" square of Background, and then to a 3-1/2" x 6-1/2" Background, building a 6-1/2" square.

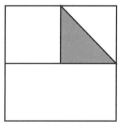

3. Make (4) Half Square Triangles with 6-1/2" squares of Color A on top of a Step 2 unit.

4. Assemble the block, sandwiching a 6-1/2" square of Background between the four units as an On Point Center Square.

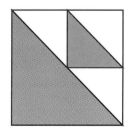

Goose & Gosling

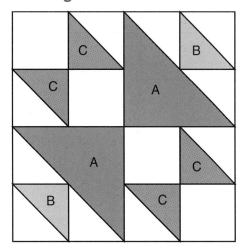

Color A
(2) 6-1/2" sq.

Color B
(2) 3-1/2" sq.

Color C
(4) 3-1/2" sq.

Background
(2) 3-1/2" x 6-1/2"
(12) 3-1/2" sq.

Folds used:
Half Square Triangles

Sequence:
1. Make (4) Half Square Triangles with 3-1/2" squares of Color C on top of 3-1/2" squares of Background.

2. Join these into two 4-patches with the additional 3-1/2" squares of Background.

3. Make (2) Half Square Triangles with 3-1/2" squares of Color B on top of 3-1/2" squares of Background.

4. Join each of these Step 3 units to a 3-1/2" square of Background and then to a 3-1/2" x 6-1/2" Background.

5. Make (2) Half Square Triangles with 6-1/2" squares of Color A on top of a Step 4 unit.

6. Assemble the block.

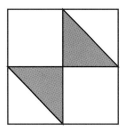
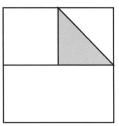
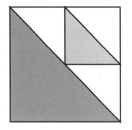

Grandpa's Favorite

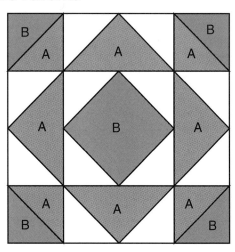

Color A
(4) 3-1/2" x 6-1/2"
(4) 3-1/2" sq.

Color B
(1) 6-1/2" sq.
(4) 3-1/2" sq.

Background
(12) 3-1/2" sq.

Folds used:
Half Square Triangle
Flying Goose
On Point Center Square

Sequence:
1. Make (4) Half Square Triangles with 3-1/2" squares of Color A on top of 3-1/2" squares of Color B.

2. Make (4) Flying Geese with 3-1/2" x 6-1/2" Color A between 3-1/2" squares of Background.

3. Make an On Point Center Square using the 6-1/2" square of Color B between 3-1/2" squares of Background.

4. Assemble the block.

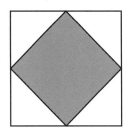

Hill & Valley

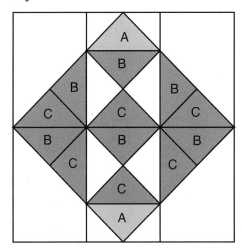

Hollis Star

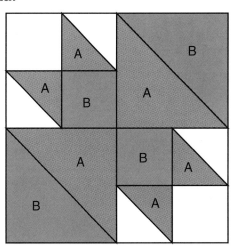

Color A
(2) 2-1/2" x 4-1/2"

Color B
(2) 4-7/8" sq.
(2) 2-1/2" x 4-1/2"

Color C
(2) 4-7/8" sq.
(2) 2-1/2" x 4-1/2"

Background
(4) 4-1/2" x 6-1/2"
(4) 2-1/2" x 4-1/2"
(4) 2-1/2" sq.

Folds used:
Pieced Half Square Triangles
Flying Goose
Nose to Nose Geese

Sequence:
1. Make (4) traditional half square triangles from the 4-7/8" squares of Color B and the 4-7/8" squares of Color C.

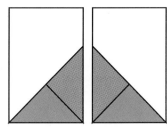

2. Place these Pieced Half Square Triangles on top of 4-1/2" x 6-1/2" Backgrounds, making (4) in two mirror image pairs.

3. Make (2) Flying Geese with 2-1/2" x 4-1/2" Color A between 2-1/2" squares of Background.

4. Make (2) Nose to Nose Geese with 2-1/2" x 4-1/2" Color B and 2-1/2" x 4-1/2" Color C between 2-1/2" x 4-1/2" Backgrounds.

5. Assemble the block.

Color A
(2) 6-1/2" sq.
(4) 3-1/2" sq.

Color B
(2) 6-1/2" sq.
(2) 3-1/2" sq.

Background
(6) 3-1/2" sq.

Folds used:
Half Square Triangle

Sequence:
1. Make (4) Half Square Triangles with 3-1/2" squares of Color A on top of 3-1/2" squares of Background.

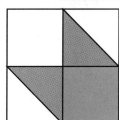

2. Join the Step 1 units into 4-patches, adding 3-1/2" squares of Color B and 3-1/2" squares of Background.

3. Make (2) Half Square Triangles with 6-1/2" squares of Color A on top of 6-1/2" squares of Color B.

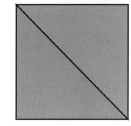

4. Assemble the block.

Hovering Hawks

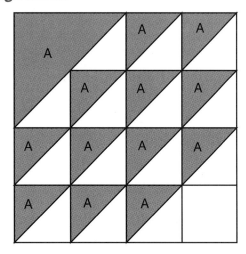

Color A
(1) 6-1/2" sq.
(12) 3-1/2" sq.

Background
(1) 3-1/2" x 6-1/2"
(14) 3-1/2" sq.

Folds used:
Half Square Triangle

Sequence:
1. Make (12) Half Square Triangles with 3-1/2" squares of Color A on top of 3-1/2" squares of Background.

2. Take (1) of the Half Square Triangles from Step 1, add a 3-1/2" square of Background, followed by a 3-1/2" x 6-1/2" Background to make it 6-1/2" square.

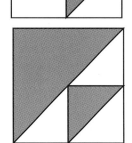

3. Make (1) Half Square Triangle with the 6-1/2" square of Color A on top of the unit made in Step 2.

4. Assemble the block.

Kansas Trouble

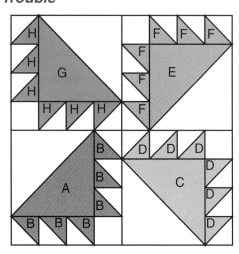

Colors A,C,E,G
(1) 5" sq.

Colors B,D,F,H
(6) 2" sq.

Background
(4) 5" sq.
(28) 2" sq.

Folds used:
Half Square Triangle

Sequence:
1. Make (1) Half Square Triangle of each of the 5" square Colors A, C, E, and G on top of a 5" square of Background.

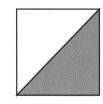

2. Make (6) Half Square Triangles of each of the 2" squares of Colors B, D, F, and H on top of 2" squares of Background.

3. Sew the Color B units with a 2" square of Background to the Color A unit as shown. Likewise join the Color D's to Color C, Color F's to Color E, and Color H's to Color G.

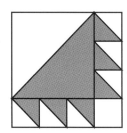

4. Assemble the block.

Mosaic

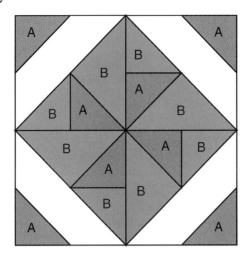

Color A
(8) 3-1/2" sq.

Color B
(8) 3-1/2" x 6-1/2"

Background
(4) 6-1/2" sq.

Folds used:
Snowball Corner
Double Half Square Triangles

Sequence:
1. Make (4) Snowball Corners with 3-1/2" squares Color A on top of and in the lower left corner of 3-1/2" x 6-1/2" Color B.

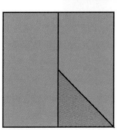

2. Stitch the Step 1 units each to another Color B 3-1/2" x 6-1/2" with a scant 1/4" seam.

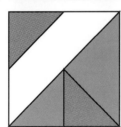

3. Make (4) Double Half Square Triangles with 6-1/2" squares of Background and then 3-1/2" squares of Color A on top of the Step 2 units as shown.

4. Assemble the block.

Pinwheel

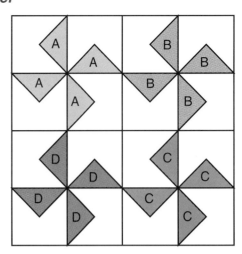

Color A
(4) 3-1/2" sq.

Color B
(4) 3-1/2" sq.

Color C
(4) 3-1/2" sq.

Color D
(4) 3-1/2" sq.

Background
(16) 3-1/2" sq.

Folds used:
Prairie Point Pinwheel

Sequence:
1. With each Color, make (4) Pinwheel parts of 3-1/2" squares of Color on top of 3-1/2" squares of Background.

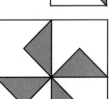

2. Join the pieces of each Color into a Pinwheel.

3. Assemble the block.

Robbing Peter to Pay Paul

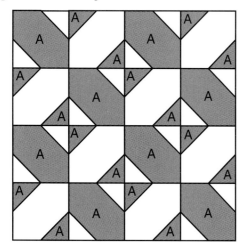

Color A
(8) 3-1/2" sq.
(16) 2" sq.

Background
(8) 3-1/2" sq.
(16) 2" sq.

Folds used:
Double Snowball Corners

Sequence:
1. Make (8) Double Snowball Corners with 2" squares of Color A on top of opposite corners of 3-1/2" squares of Background.

2. Make (8) Double Snowball Corners with 2" squares of Background on top of opposite corners of 3-1/2" squares of Color A.

3. Assemble the block.

Rolling Pinwheel

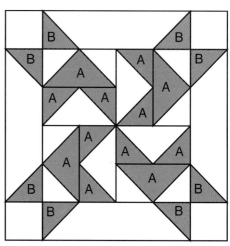

Color A
(4) 2-1/2" x 4-1/2"
(8) 2-1/2" sq.

Color B
(8) 2-1/2" sq.

Background
(4) 2-1/2" x 8-1/2"
(4) 2-1/2" x 4-1/2"
(12) 2-1/2" sq.

Folds used:
Double Snowball Corner
Flying Goose

Sequence:
1. Make (4) Double Snowball Corners with 2-1/2" squares of Color A on top of 2-1/2" x 4-1/2" Backgrounds.

2. Make (4) Flying Geese using 2-1/2" x 4-1/2" Color A between 2-1/2" squares of Background.

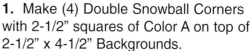

3. Join the Step 1 units to the Step 2 units, keeping the direction as shown, with scant 1/4" seams.

4. Make (4) Double Snowball Corners with 2-1/2" squares of Color B on top of 2-1/2" x 8-1/2" Backgrounds.

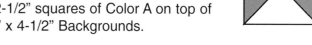

5. Assemble the block.

Salem

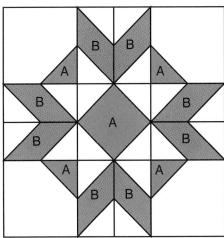

Color A
(1) 4-1/2" sq.
(4) 2-1/2" sq.

Color B
(8) 2-1/2" x 4-1/2"

Background
(4) 4-1/2" sq.
(8) 2-1/2" x 4-1/2"
(12) 2-1/2" sq.

Folds used:
On Point Center Square
Star Points with Snowball Corners

Sequence:

1. Make an On Point Center Square with the 4-1/2" square of Color A between 2-1/2" squares of Background.

2. Make (4) mirror image pairs of Star Points using 2-1/2" x 4-1/2" Color B on top of 2-1/2" x 4-1/2" Backgrounds.

3. Snowball 2-1/2" squares of Background on top of the Step 2 units.

4. Join the mirror image pairs with scant 1/4" seams.

5. Make (4) Snowball Corners using 2-1/2" squares of Color A on top of 4-1/2" squares of Background.

6. Assemble the block.

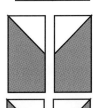

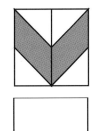

Seesaw

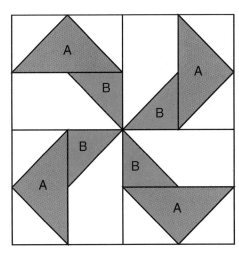

Color A
(4) 3-1/2" x 6-1/2"

Color B
(4) 3-1/2" sq.

Background
(4) 3-1/2" x 6-1/2"
(8) 3-1/2" sq.

Folds used:
Snowball Corner
Flying Goose

Sequence:

1. Make (4) Snowball Corners with 3-1/2" squares of Color B on top of 3-1/2" x 6-1/2" Backgrounds.

2. Make (4) Flying Geese with 3-1/2" x 6-1/2" Color A between 3-1/2" squares of Background.

3. Sew each Step 1 unit to a Step 2 unit, with a scant 1/4" seam, as shown.

4. Assemble the block.

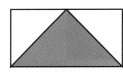

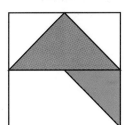

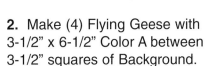

21

Square and Star

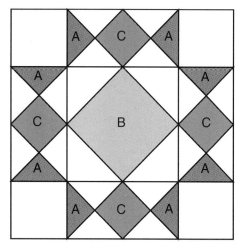

Color A
(8) 2" x 3-1/2"

Color B
(1) 6-1/2" sq.

Color C
(4) 3-1/2" sq.

Background
(8) 3-1/2" sq.
(16) 2" x 3-1/2"

Folds used:
On Point Center Square
Center Square with Geese

Sequence:
1. Make an On Point Center Square with the 6-1/2" square of Color B between 3-1/2" squares of Background.

2. Make (4) Center Squares with Geese using 3-1/2" squares of Color C and 2" x 3-1/2" of Color A between 2" x 3-1/2" Backgrounds.

3. Assemble the block.

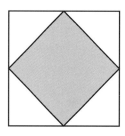

T Block

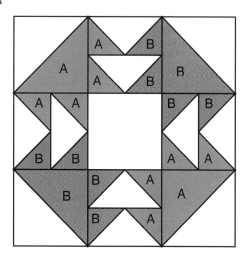

Color A
(2) 4-1/2" sq.
(8) 2-1/2" sq.

Color B
(2) 4-1/2" sq.
(8) 2-1/2" sq.

Background
(5) 4-1/2" sq.
(8) 2-1/2" x 4-1/2"

Folds used:
Half Square Triangle
Double Snowball Corners

Sequence:
1. Make (2) Half Square Triangles of 4-1/2" squares of Color A on top of 4-1/2" squares of Background. Likewise make (2) Half Square Triangles of 4-1/2" squares of Color B on top of 4-1/2" squares of Background.

2. Make (4) Double Snowball Corners using 2-1/2" squares of Color A on the left and 2-1/2" squares of Color B on the right, both on top of 2-1/2" x 4-1/2" Backgrounds.

3. Join the Step 2 units in pairs facing the same direction with scant 1/4" seams.

4. Make (4) Double Snowball Corners using 2-1/2" squares of Color B on the left and 2-1/2" squares of Color A on the right, both on top of 2-1/2" x 4-1/2" Backgrounds.

5. Join the Step 5 units in pairs facing the same direction with scant 1/4" seams.

6. Assemble the block.

Turkey Tracks

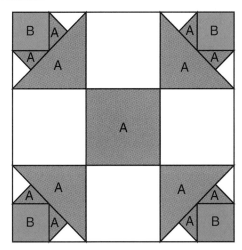

Color A
(5) 4-1/2" sq.
(12) 2-1/2" sq.

Color B
(4) 2-1/2" sq.

Background
(4) 4-1/2" sq.
(8) 2-1/2" sq.

Folds used:
Tulip Tip

Sequence:
1. Make (8) Half Square Triangles to begin a Tulip Tip fold with 2-1/2" squares of Color A on top of 2-1/2" squares of Background.

2. Assemble (4) 4-patch units with Step 1 pieces, the remaining 2-1/2" squares of Color A, and 2-1/2" squares of Color B.

3. Make (4) Tulip Tips with the Step 2 units under folded 4-1/2" squares of Color A.

4. Assemble the block.

Ultimate 3-D Star

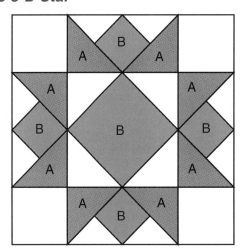

Color A
(8) 3-1/2" sq.

Color B
(5) 6-1/2" sq.

Background
(4) 3-1/2" x 6-1/2"
(8) 3-1/2" sq.

Folds Used:
On Point Center Square
Crocus with Snowballs

Sequence:
1. Make an On Point Center Square with a 6-1/2" square Color B between 3-1/2" squares of Background.

2. Make (4) Crocus with Snowballs using 6-1/2" squares of Color B and then 3-1/2" squares of Color A on top of 3-1/2" x 6-1/2" Backgrounds.

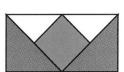

3. Assemble the block.

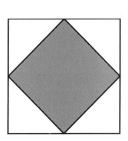

Union

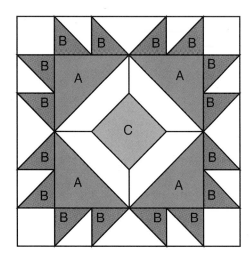

Color A
(4) 4-1/2" sq.

Color B
(16) 2-1/2" sq.

Color C
(1) 4-1/2" sq.

Background
(4) 4-1/2" sq.
(4) 2-1/2" x 4-1/2"
(12) 2-1/2" sq.

Folds used:
Half Square Triangle
On Point Center Square
Snowball Corners

Sequence:
1. Make (4) Half Square Triangles of 4-1/2" squares of Color A on top of 4-1/2" squares of Background.

2. Join these with a 4-1/2" square of Color C On Point Center Square between the Step 1 units.

3. Make (8) Half Square Triangles of 2-1/2" squares of Color B on top of 2-1/2" squares of Background.

4. Make (4) Snowball Corners of 2-1/2" squares of Color B on top of 2-1/2" x 4-1/2" Backgrounds.

5. Add a Half Square Triangle from Step 3 to each end of the Step 4 Snowball Corners.

6. Assemble the block.

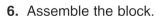

Union Square

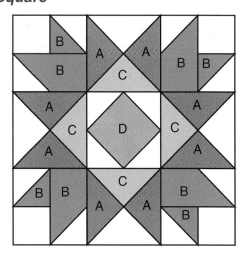

Color A
(8) 2-1/2" x 4-1/2"

Color B
(4) 2-1/2" x 4-1/2"
(4) 2-1/2" sq.

Color C
(4) 2-1/2" x 4-1/2"

Color D
(1) 4-1/2" sq.

Background
(4) 2-1/2" x 4-1/2"
(16) 2-1/2" sq.

Folds used:
Short Sheet Fold
Half Square Triangle
Nose to Nose Geese
On Point Center Square

Sequence:
1. Make (4) Short Sheet Folds of 2-1/2" x 4-1/2" Color B and 2-1/2" squares of Background.
2. Make (4) Half Square Triangles of 2-1/2" squares of Color B and 2-1/2" squares of Background.
3. Stitch each Half Square Triangle from Step 2 to a 2-1/2" square of Background as shown. Attach the Short Sheet Folds from Step 1 to this unit, using scant 1/4" seams.
4. Make (4) Nose to Nose Geese with 2-1/2" x 4-1/2" Color A sandwiched between a 2-1/2" x 4-1/2" Background and a 2-1/2" x 4-1/2" Color C.
5. Make an On Point Center Square of a 4-1/2" square Color D between 2-1/2" squares of Background.
6. Assemble the block.

Weathervane

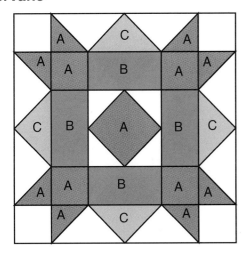

Color A
(1) 4-1/2" sq.
(12) 2-1/2" sq.

Color B
(4) 2-1/2" x 4-1/2"

Color C
(4) 2-1/2" x 4-1/2"

Background
(8) 2-1/2" x 4-1/2"
(8) 2-1/2" sq.

Folds used:
Goose with Snowballs
On Point Center Square

Sequence:
1. Make (4) Goose with Snowballs with 2-1/2" x 4-1/2" Color C between 2-1/2" x 4-1/2" Backgrounds and with 2-1/2" squares of Color A on top.

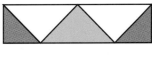

2. Make an On Point Center Square of a 4-1/2" square of Color A between 2-1/2" squares of Background.

3. Assemble the block.

Note: The center section surrounding the On Point Center Square is standard flat piecing.

Wheels

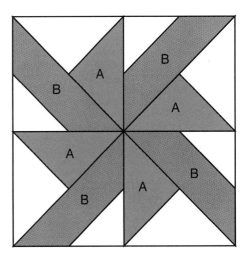

Color A
(4) 6-1/2" sq.

Color B
(4) 6-1/2" sq.

Background
(4) 6-1/2" sq.
(4) 3-1/2" sq.

Folds used:
Overlapping Half Square Triangles

Sequence:
1. Make (4) Half Square Triangles with 6-1/2" squares of Color A on top of 6-1/2" squares of Background.

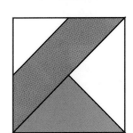

2. Make Overlapping Half Square Triangles using Step 1 units under 6-1/2" squares of Color B and 3-1/2" squares of Background.

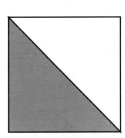

3. Assemble the block.

Windblown Square

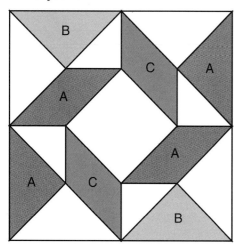

Color A
(4) 3-1/2" x 6-1/2"

Color B
(2) 3-1/2" x 6-1/2"

Color C
(2) 3-1/2" x 6-1/2"

Background
(1) 6-1/2" sq.
(4) 3-1/2" x 6-1/2"
(4) 3-1/2" sq.

Folds used:
Flying Goose with Star Point
On Point Center Square

Sequence:
1. Make (2) Flying Geese with Star Points using 3-1/2" x 6-1/2" Color A between a 3-1/2" square and a 3-1/2" x 6-1/2" Background.

2. Finish these Star Points by adding a 3-1/2" x 6-1/2" Color C to the Step 1 units.

3. Make (2) Flying Geese with Star Points using 3-1/2" x 6-1/2" Color B between a 3-1/2" square and a 3-1/2" x 6-1/2" Background.

4 Finish these Star Points by adding a 3-1/2" x 6-1/2" Color A to the Step 3 units.

5. Join these four parts with an On point Center Square of the 6-1/2" square of Background.

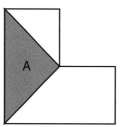

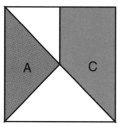

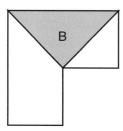

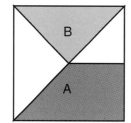

Yankee Puzzle

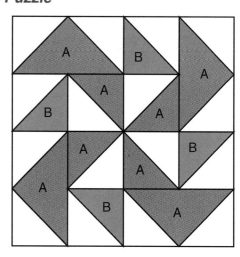

Color A
(4) 3-1/2" x 6-1/2"
(4) 3-1/2" sq.

Color B
(4) 3-1/2" sq.

Background
(16) 3-1/2" sq.

Folds used:
Half Square Triangle
Flying Goose

Sequence:
1. Make (4) Half Square Triangles of 3-1/2" squares of Color A on top of 3-1/2" squares of Background.

2. Make (4) Half Square Triangles using 3-1/2" squares of Color B on top of 3-1/2" squares of Background.

3. Sew the Step 1 and Step 2 pieces together as shown.

4. Make (4) Flying Geese with 3-1/2" x 6-1/2" Color A between 3-1/2" squares of Background.

5. Join the Geese to the Step 3 units.

6. Assemble the block.

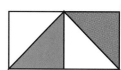

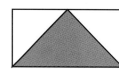

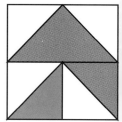

Set the Blocks into a Quilt

Select either a Straight Set or an On Point Set for your blocks. Yardages are provided for a range of sizes in either set. These yardage requirements are 10% greater than the minimum amount needed, to allow 3% shrinkage and a 7% "goof" factor.

Straight Set *(back cover)*

YARDAGE

These yardages are for the SET ONLY. Be certain to purchase yardage for your blocks based on the information provided on page 2!

Size	# of Blocks	Background	# of Setting Star Colors & yardage for EACH	Binding	Backing
44" x 60"	6	1-3/4 yards	Four - 1/4 yard each	1/2 yard	2-3/4 yards
44" x 76"	8	2-1/4 yards	Five - 1/4 yard each	5/8 yard	2-3/4 yards
60" x 76"	12	2-7/8 yards	Five - 1/3 yard each	5/8 yard	3-3/4 yards
76" x 92"	20	4-1/4 yards	Six - 1/3 yard each	3/4 yard	5-1/2 yards*

*fabric must be at least 40" wide after pretreating

CUTTING

# of Blocks	EACH of the Setting Stars	Background	Binding
6	(3) 4-1/2" squares (24) 2-1/2" squares	(11) 4-1/2" strips into: (27) 4-1/2" x 12-1/2" (18) 4-1/2" sq. (3) 2-1/2" strips into: (48) 2-1/2" sq.	(6) 2-1/2" strips
8	(3) 4-1/2" sq. (24) 2-1/2" sq.	(14) 4-1/2" strips into: (34) 4-1/2" x 12-1/2" (20) 4-1/2" sq. (4) 2-1/2" strips into: (60) 2-1/2" sq.	(7) 2-1/2" strips
12	(4) 4-1/2" sq. (32) 2-1/2" sq.	(18) 4-1/2" strips into: (45) 4-1/2" x 12-1/2" (22) 4-1/2" sq. (5) 2-1/2" strips into: (80) 2-1/2" sq.	(8) 2-1/2" strips
20	(5) 4-1/2" sq. (40) 2-1/2" sq.	(26) 4-1/2" strips into: (67) 4-1/2" x 12-1/2" (26) 4-1/2" sq. (8) 2-1/2" strips into: (120) 2-1/2" sq.	(9) 2-1/2" strips

Straight Set Construction

1. Lay the blocks out in the desired positions.

2. Make On Point Center Squares of each of the designated Setting Star Colors using the 4-1/2" squares of all the Colors and (4) 2-1/2" squares of Background for each.

3. Position these On Point Center Squares between the blocks, at the corners.

4. Also position the 4-1/2" x 12-1/2" Background pieces between the blocks, and around the outer edges of the blocks. Notice the second round of these rectangles around the outside of the entire quilt.

5. Position the 4-1/2" squares of Background around the outer edge.

6. Using the On Point Center Squares to show Color Placement, stitch (2) Snowball Corners of the correct color at each end of each 4-1/2" x 12-1/2" rectangle.

7. Also sew the correct Color Snowball Corners to the 4-1/2" squares which extend into the outer row.

8. Carefully stitch the quilt together. The best way I've found when working with sashing, is to sew the sashing and cornerstone blocks to the left and top edges of each of the blocks.

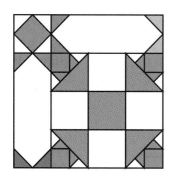

9. The blocks along the right edge also have sashing sewn to their right edge.

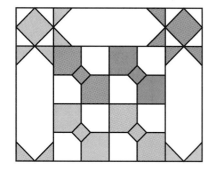

10. The blocks along the lower edge also have sashing sewn to their bottom edge.

11. The block in the lower right corner will be surrounded!

12. Add the outer round of border pieces.

13. Press gingerly so not to smash the Three Dimensional effect!

14. Layer and quilt.

15. Bind.

On Point Set (*front cover*)
YARDAGE
These yardages are for the SET ONLY. Be certain to purchase yardage for your blocks based on the information provided on page 2!

Size	# of Blocks	Background	# of Setting Star Colors & yardage for EACH	Border Stripe	Binding	Backing
67-1/2" x 90"	8	5 yards	Six - 1/4 yard each	1/3 yard	5/8 yard	5-1/2 yards
90" x 90"	13	6-1/8 yards	Six - 1/3 yard each	3/8 yard	3/4 yard	8-1/4 yards
90" x 112-1/2"	18	7-1/2 yards	Six - 3/8 yard each	1/2 yard	7/8 yard	8-1/4 yards

CUTTING

# of Blocks	EACH of the Setting Stars	Background	Border Stripe	Binding

8	(3) 4-1/2" sq.
	(24) 2-1/2" sq.
		(3) 14" strips into:
		(5) 14" squares
		(1) 12-1/2" square
		(2) 11" squares
		(3) 12-1/2" strips into:
		    (9) 12-1/2" squares
		(12) 4-1/2" strips into:
		    (24) 4-1/2" x 12-1/2
		    (30) 4-1/2" sq.
		(5) 2-1/2" strips into:
		    (68) 2-1/2" sq.
		(8) 2" strips for outer border
			(8) 1-1/4" strips	(8) 2-1/2" strips

13	(4) 4-1/2" sq.
	(32) 2-1/2" sq.
		(3) 14" strips into:
		(6) 14" squares
		(2) 11" squares
		(4) 12-1/2" strips into:
		    (12) 12-1/2" squares
		(16) 4-1/2" strips into:
		    (36) 4-1/2" x 12-1/2"
		    (36) 4-1/2" sq.
		(6) 2-1/2" strips into:
		    (96) 2-1/2" sq.
		(9) 2" strips for outer border
			(9) 1-1/4" strips	(9) 2-1/2" strips

18	(6) 4-1/2" sq.
	(48) 2-1/2" sq.
		(4) 14" strips into:
		(7) 14" squares
		(2) 11" squares
		(2) 12-1/2" squares
		(4) 12-1/2" strips into:
		    (12) 12-1/2" squares
		(21) 4-1/2" strips into:
		    (48) 4-1/2" x 12-1/2"
		    (42) 4-1/2" sq.
		(8) 2-1/2" strips into:
		    (124) 2-1/2" sq.
		(11) 2" strips for outer border
			(11) 1-1/4" strips	(11) 2-1/2" strips

On Point Set Construction

1. Lay blocks out in the desired positions.

2. Place plain 12-1/2" squares around the outer edges.

3. Make On Point Center Squares of each of the Setting Star Colors using the 4-1/2" squares of Color and (4) 2-1/2" squares of Background for each.
Note: In the 8 block set, a total of 17 stars are needed. In the 18 block set, a total of 31 stars are needed.

4. Position these On Point Center Squares between the blocks, at the corners.

5. Also position the 4-1/2" x 12-1/2" Background pieces between the blocks, and the 4-1/2" squares around the edges of the quilt.

6. The 14" squares of Background are cut in fourths like an "X" and placed around the four sides of the quilt.

7. The (2) 11" squares of Background are cut in half, diagonally, and placed in the four corners.

8. Using the On Point Center Squares to show Color Placement, stitch (2) Snowball Corners of the correct color at each end of each 4-1/2" x 12-1/2" rectangle.

9. Also sew the correct Color Snowball Corners to the 4-1/2" squares which need to be positioned around the outer edge.

10. Stitch the quilt together, in pairs of rows which include a row of blocks and a row of sashing. The diagonal units at each end will complete the paired rows.

11. After joining all the pairs of rows, trim the outer edges carefully, to square up the quilt, trimming 1/4" beyond the outer squares surrounding the setting stars.

12. Stitch the Border Stripe pieces together and add to the quilt.

13. Stitch the Outer Border pieces together and add to the quilt.

14. Layer and quilt.

15. Bind.

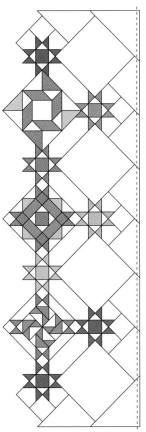

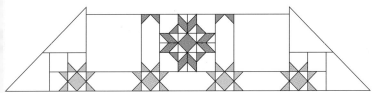

Note: The row of blocks in the exact center will not be joined with a sashing.